Good Housekeeping

D0866031

Cook it tonight!

Easy Family Meals

COLLINS & BROWN

Recipes

Quick & Easy Carbonara	4
Easy Pea Soup	6
Quick Crab Cakes	8
Chicken Chow Mein	10
Courgettes & Capers Ribbon Pasta	12
Falafel & Soured Cream Wraps	14
Thai Green Curry	16
Basil & Lemon Chicken	18
Cannellini Bean & Tomato Salad	20
Prawn, Courgette & Leek Risotto	22
Fast Fish Soup	24
Pesto Gnocchi	26
Quick Fish & Chips	28
Mauritian Vegetable Curry	30
Pork, Chilli & Mango Stir-Fry	32
Chilli Steak & Corn on the Cob	34
Easy Chicken Casserole	36
Orange & Chicken Salad	38
Mushroom, Bacon & Leek Risotto	40
Speedy Beef Noodles	42
Aubergine Parmigiana	44
Pumpkin with Chickpeas	46
Egg & Bacon Tarts	48
Poached Thai Salmon	50
Chicken with Spicy Couscous	52
Smoked Fish Pie	54
Mozzarella, Ham & Rocket Pizza	56
Chicken Fajitas	58
Potato & Chorizo Tortilla	60
Sticky Chicken Thighs	62

Quick & Easy Carbonara

shopping list

- ☐ 350g (12oz) tagliatelle
- ☐ 150g (5oz) smoked bacon, chopped
- ☐ 1 tbsp olive oil
- ☐ 2 large egg yolks

Serves 4

Preparation Time
5 minutes

Cooking Time
10 minutes

- 150ml (¼ pint) double cream
- 50g (2oz) freshly grated Parmesan
- 2 tbsp freshly chopped parsley

How to cook

1. Bring a large pan of water to the boil. Add the pasta, bring back to the boil and cook for 4 minutes or according to the pack instructions.

2. Meanwhile, fry the bacon in the olive oil for 4–5 minutes. Add to the drained pasta and keep hot

3. Put the egg yolks in a bowl and add the cream. Whisk together. Add to the pasta with the Parmesan and parsley. Toss well and serve.

Easy Pea Soup

 shopping list

☐ 1 small baguette, thinly sliced
☐ 2 tbsp basil-infused olive oil, plus extra to drizzle

Serves 4

Preparation Time
2 minutes, plus thawing

Cooking Time
15 minutes

- 450g (1lb) frozen peas, thawed
- 600ml (1 pint) vegetable stock
- salt and ground black pepper

How to cook

1. Preheat the oven to 220°C (200°C fan oven) mark 7. To make the croûtes, put the bread on a baking sheet, drizzle with 2 tbsp oil and bake for 10–15 minutes until golden.

2. Meanwhile, put the peas in a food processor, add the stock and season with salt and pepper. Blend for 2–3 minutes.

3. Pour the soup into a pan and bring to the boil, then reduce the heat and simmer for 10 minutes. Spoon into warmed bowls, add the croûtes, drizzle with extra oil and sprinkle with salt and pepper. Serve immediately.

Quick Crab Cakes

Shopping list

- [ ] 200g (7oz) fresh crabmeat
- [ ] 2 spring onions, finely chopped
- [ ] 2 red chillies, seeded and finely chopped
- [ ] finely grated zest of 1 lime
- [ ] 4 tbsp freshly chopped coriander

Serves 4

Preparation Time
15 minutes

Cooking Time
6 minutes

- about 40g (1 1/2 oz) wholemeal breadcrumbs
- 1 tbsp groundnut oil
- 1 tbsp plain flour
- salt and ground black pepper
- thinly sliced red chilli, seeds removed, to garnish
- 1 lime, cut into wedges, and salad leaves to serve

How to cook

1 Put the crabmeat in a bowl, then mix with the spring onions, chillies, lime zest, coriander and seasoning. Add enough breadcrumbs to hold the mixture together, then form into four small patties.

2 Heat 1/2 tbsp groundnut oil in a pan. Dredge the patties with flour and fry on one side for 3 minutes. Add the remaining oil, then turn the patties over and fry for a further 2–3 minutes. Garnish the crab cakes with thinly sliced red chilli and serve with lime wedges to squeeze over them, and salad leaves.

Cook's Tip
Chillies vary enormously in strength, from quite mild to blisteringly hot, depending on the type of chilli and its ripeness. Taste a small piece first to check it's not too hot for you.

Chicken Chow Mein

shopping list

- ☐ 250g (9oz) medium egg noodles
- ☐ 1 tbsp toasted sesame oil
- ☐ 2 skinless chicken breasts, cut into thin strips
- ☐ 1 bunch of spring onions, thinly sliced diagonally
- ☐ 150g (5oz) mangetouts, thickly sliced diagonally

Serves 4

Preparation Time
10 minutes

Cooking Time
10 minutes

- 125g (4oz) bean sprouts
- 100g (3½oz) cooked ham, shredded
- 120g sachet chow mein sauce
- salt and ground black pepper
- light soy sauce to serve

How to cook

1 Cook the noodles in boiling water for 4 minutes or according to the packet instructions. Drain, rinse thoroughly in cold water, drain again and set aside.

2 Meanwhile, heat a wok or large frying pan until hot, then add the oil. Add the chicken and stir-fry over a high heat for 3–4 minutes until browned all over. Add the spring onions and mangetouts, stir-fry for 2 minutes, then stir in the bean sprouts and ham and cook for a further 2 minutes.

3 Add the drained noodles, then pour in the chow mein sauce and toss together to coat evenly. Stir-fry for 2 minutes or until piping hot. Season with salt and pepper and serve immediately with light soy sauce to drizzle over.

Courgettes & Capers Ribbon Pasta

shopping list

- 450g (1lb) dried pappardelle pasta
- 2 large courgettes, coarsely grated
- 50g can anchovies in oil, drained and roughly chopped
- 1 red chilli, seeded and finely chopped
- 2 tbsp salted capers, rinsed

Serves 4

Preparation Time
5 minutes

Cooking Time
10–15 minutes

- 1 garlic clove, crushed
- 4 tbsp pitted black kalamata olives, roughly chopped
- 4 tbsp extra virgin olive oil
- 2 tbsp freshly chopped flat-leafed parsley

How to cook

1. To save time, prepare the other ingredients while the pasta is cooking. Cook the pappardelle in a large pan of lightly salted boiling water according to the packet instructions. About 1 minute before the end of the cooking time, add the courgette, then simmer until the pasta is al dente.

2. Meanwhile, put the anchovies into a small pan over a low heat. Add the chilli, capers, garlic, olives and olive oil and cook, stirring, for 2–3 minutes.

3. Drain the pasta and put back in the pan. Pour the hot anchovy mixture on top, mix well and toss through the parsley. Season with salt and pepper, and serve immediately.

Falafel & Soured Cream Wraps

shopping list

- ☐ 6 large flour tortillas
- ☐ 200g (7oz) soured cream
- ☐ 100g (3½oz) wild rocket
- ☐ a small handful of fresh coriander, chopped

Serves 6

Preparation Time
5 minutes, plus
chilling

- 1 celery stick, finely chopped
- 180g pack ready-made falafel, roughly chopped or crumbled

How to cook

1 Lay the tortillas on a board and spread each one with a little soured cream.

2 Divide the rocket among the wraps and sprinkle with coriander, celery and falafel.

3 Roll up as tightly as you can, then wrap each roll in clingfilm and chill for up to 3 hours or until ready to use. To serve, unwrap and cut each roll into quarters.

Thai Green Curry

Shopping list

- [ ] 2 tsp vegetable oil
- [ ] 1 green chilli, seeded and finely chopped
- [ ] 4cm (1½ in) piece fresh root ginger, peeled and finely grated
- [ ] 1 lemongrass stalk, cut into 3 pieces
- [ ] 225g (8oz) brown-cap or oyster mushrooms

Serves 6

Preparation Time
10 minutes

Cooking Time
15 minutes

- 1 tbsp Thai green curry paste
- 300ml (½ pint) coconut milk
- 150ml (¼ pint) chicken stock
- 1 tbsp Thai fish sauce
- 1 tsp light soy sauce

- 350g (12oz) skinless chicken breasts, cut into bite-sized pieces
- 350g (12oz) cooked and peeled large prawns
- fresh coriander sprigs to garnish
- rice to serve

How to cook

1 Heat the oil in a wok or large frying pan, add the chilli, ginger, lemongrass and mushrooms and stir-fry for about 3 minutes or until the mushrooms begin to turn golden. Add the curry paste and fry for a further minute.

2 Pour in the coconut milk, stock, fish sauce and soy sauce and bring to the boil. Stir in the chicken and simmer for about 8 minutes or until the chicken is cooked. Add the prawns and cook for a further minute to heat through. Garnish with coriander sprigs and serve with rice.

Basil & Lemon Chicken

shopping list

- grated zest of 1 lemon, plus 4 tbsp lemon juice
- 1 tsp caster sugar
- 1 tsp Dijon mustard
- 175ml (6fl oz) lemon-infused oil
- 4 tbsp freshly chopped basil

Serves 4

Preparation Time
15 minutes,
plus 15 minutes
marinating

- 2 x 210g packs roast chicken
- 250g (9oz) baby leaf spinach
- 55g pack crisp bacon, broken into small pieces
- salt and ground black pepper

How to cook

1. Put the lemon zest and juice, sugar, mustard and oil in a small bowl. Season with salt and pepper. Whisk together until thoroughly combined, then add the basil.

2. Remove any bones from the roast chicken, leave the skin attached and slice into five or six pieces. Arrange the sliced chicken in a dish and pour the dressing over, then cover and leave to marinate for at least 15 minutes.

3. Just before serving, lift the chicken from the dressing and put to one side.

4. Put the spinach in a large bowl, pour the dressing over and toss together. Arrange the chicken on top of the spinach, and sprinkle with the bacon. Serve immediately.

Cannellini Bean & Tomato Salad

shopping list

- ½ red onion, very finely sliced
- 2 tbsp red wine vinegar
- a small handful each of freshly chopped mint and flat-leafed parsley
- 2 x 400g cans cannellini beans, drained and rinsed

Serves 6

Preparation Time
5 minutes,
plus 30 minutes
marinating

- 4 tbsp extra virgin olive oil
- 4 celery sticks, sliced
- 75g (3oz) sunblush tomatoes,
  snipped in half
- salt and ground black pepper

How to cook

1. Put the onion into a small bowl, add the vinegar and toss. Leave to marinate for 30 minutes – this stage is important as it takes the astringency out of the onion.

2. Tip the onion and vinegar into a large bowl, add the remaining ingredients, season with salt and pepper and toss everything together.

Cook's Tip
Save money and replace the tinned cannellini beans with 200g dried beans. Soak and cook according to the packet instructions.

Prawn, Courgette & Leek Risotto

shopping list

- [ ] 1 tbsp olive oil
- [ ] 25g (1oz) butter
- [ ] 1 leek, finely chopped
- [ ] 2 courgettes, thinly sliced
- [ ] 2 garlic cloves, crushed
- [ ] 350g (12oz) arborio rice

Serves 6

Preparation Time
10 minutes

Cooking Time
30 minutes

- 100ml (3½ fl oz) dry white wine
- 1.6 litres (2¾ pints) vegetable stock
- 200g (7oz) cooked and peeled prawns
- small bunch parsley or mint, or a mixture of both, chopped
- salt and ground black pepper

How to cook

1. Heat the oil and half the butter in a large shallow pan. Add the leek, courgettes and garlic and soften over a low heat. Add the rice and cook, stirring well, for 1 minute, then pour in the wine. Let bubble until the wine has evaporated.

2. Meanwhile, in another large pan, heat the stock to a steady, low simmer. Add a ladleful of the stock to the rice and simmer, stirring, until absorbed. Continue adding the stock, a ladleful at a time.

3. When nearly all the stock has been added and the rice is al dente (just tender but with a little bite at the centre), add the prawns. Season to taste and stir in the remaining stock and the rest of the butter. Stir through and take off the heat. Cover and leave to stand for a couple of minutes, then stir the chopped herbs through it Serve immediately.

Fast Fish Soup

shopping list

- [ ] 1 leek, finely sliced
- [ ] 4 fat garlic cloves, crushed
- [ ] 3 celery sticks, finely sliced
- [ ] 1 small fennel bulb, finely sliced
- [ ] 1 red chilli, seeded and finely chopped

Serves 4

Preparation Time
10 minutes

Cooking Time
15 minutes

- 3 tbsp olive oil
- 50ml (2fl oz) dry white wine
- about 750g (1lb 10oz) mixed fish and shellfish, such as haddock, monkfish, salmon, raw shelled prawns and cleaned mussels

- 4 medium tomatoes, chopped
- 2 tbsp freshly chopped thyme
- salt and ground black pepper

How to cook

1 Put the leek in a large pan and add the garlic, celery, fennel, chilli and olive oil. Cook over a medium heat for 5 minutes or until the vegetables are soft and beginning to colour.

2 Stir in 1.1 litres (2 pints) boiling water and the wine. Bring to the boil, then simmer the soup, covered, for 5 minutes.

3 Meanwhile, cut the fish into large chunks. Add to the soup with the tomatoes and thyme. Continue simmering gently until the fish has just turned opaque. Add the prawns and simmer for 1 minute then add the mussels – if you're using them. As soon as all the mussels have opened, season the soup and ladle into warmed bowls. Discard any mussels that remain closed, then serve immediately.

Pesto Gnocchi

shopping list

- 800g (1lb 12oz) fresh gnocchi
- 200g (7oz) green beans, trimmed and chopped
- 125g (4oz) fresh green pesto
- 10 sunblush tomatoes, roughly chopped

Serves 4

Preparation Time
10 minutes

Cooking Time
10 minutes

How to cook

1. Cook the gnocchi in a large pan of lightly salted boiling water according to the packet instructions. Add the beans to the water for the last 3 minutes of cooking time.

2. Drain the gnocchi and beans and put back in the pan. Add the pesto and tomatoes and toss well. Serve immediately.

Cook's Tip
Like pasta, these little dumplings made from potatoes, flour and egg, are an Italian staple and are just as quick and easy to cook. Just wait for them to bob to the surface of the water, give them one more minute and they're ready to toss with a sauce of your choice.

Quick Fish & Chips

shopping list

- 4 litres (7 pints) sunflower oil for deep-frying
- 125g (4oz) self-raising flour
- ¼ tsp baking powder
- ¼ tsp salt
- 1 medium egg
- 150ml (¼ pint) sparkling mineral water

Serves 2

Preparation Time
15 minutes

Cooking Time
12 minutes

- 2 hake fillets, about 125g (4oz) each
- 450g (1lb) Desirée potatoes, cut into 1cm (½ in) chips
- salt, vinegar and garlic mayonnaise to serve

How to cook

1 Heat the oil in a deep-fryer to 190°C (test by frying a small cube of bread; it should brown in 20 seconds).

2 Whiz the flour, baking powder, salt, egg and water in a food processor until combined into a batter. Remove the blade from the food processor. Alternatively, put the ingredients in a bowl and beat everything together until smooth. Drop one of the fish fillets into the batter to coat it.

3 Put half the chips in the deep-fryer, then add the battered fish. Fry for 6 minutes or until just cooked, then remove and drain well on kitchen paper. Keep warm if not serving immediately.

4 Drop the remaining fillet into the batter to coat, then repeat step 3 with the remaining chips. Serve with salt, vinegar and garlic mayonnaise.

Mauritian Vegetable Curry

Shopping list

- [ ] 3 tbsp vegetable oil
- [ ] 1 onion, finely sliced
- [ ] 4 garlic cloves, crushed
- [ ] 2.5cm (1in) piece fresh root ginger, peeled and grated
- [ ] 3 tbsp medium curry powder
- [ ] 6 fresh curry leaves

Serves 4

Preparation Time
15 minutes

Cooking Time
25–30 minutes

- 150g (5oz) potato, peeled and cut into 1cm (½in) cubes
- 125g (4oz) aubergine, cut into 2cm (1in) sticks, 5mm (¼in) wide
- 150g (5oz) carrots, peeled and cut into 5mm (¼in) dice
- 900ml (1½ pints) vegetable stock
- pinch of saffron threads
- 150g (5oz) green beans, trimmed
- 75g (3oz) frozen peas
- salt and ground black pepper
- 3 tbsp chopped fresh coriander to garnish

How to cook

1 Heat the oil in a large heavy-based pan over a low heat. Add the onion and fry for 5–10 minutes until golden. Add the garlic, ginger, curry powder and curry leaves and fry for a further minute.

2 Add the potato and aubergine to the pan and fry, stirring, for 2 minutes. Add the carrots, stock and saffron. Season with plenty of salt and pepper. Cover and cook for 10 minutes until the potato and carrots are almost tender.

3 Add the beans and peas to the pan and cook for a further 4 minutes. Sprinkle with the chopped coriander and serve.

Pork, Chilli & Mango Stir-fry

shopping list

- ⬚ 75g (3oz) medium egg noodles
- ⬚ 1 tsp groundnut oil
- ⬚ ½ red chilli, seeded and finely chopped
- ⬚ 125g (4oz) pork stir-fry strips

Serves 4

Preparation Time
5 minutes

Cooking Time
about 10 minutes

- 1 head pak choi, roughly chopped
- 1 tbsp soy sauce
- ½ ripe mango, peeled and sliced

How to cook

1 Bring a large pan of water to the boil and cook the noodles according to the instructions on the packet. Drain, then plunge into cold water and put to one side.

2 Meanwhile, heat the oil in a wok or large frying pan until very hot. Add the chilli and pork and stir-fry for 3–4 minutes. Add the pak choi and soy sauce and cook for a further 2–3 minutes. Add the mango and toss to combine.

3 Drain the noodles and add them to the pan. Toss well and cook for 1–2 minutes until heated through. Serve immediately.

Chilli Steak & Corn on the Cob

shopping list

- 50g (2oz) butter, softened
- 1 large red chilli, seeded and finely chopped
- 1 garlic clove, crushed
- 25g (1oz) freshly grated Parmesan

Serves 4

Preparation Time
5 minutes

Cooking Time
15 minutes

- [ ] 1 tbsp finely chopped fresh basil
- [ ] 4 corn on the cob, each cut into three
- [ ] 1 tbsp olive oil
- [ ] 4 sirloin steaks, about 150g (5oz) each

How to cook

1. Put the butter in a bowl and beat with a wooden spoon. Add the chilli, garlic, Parmesan and basil, and mix everything together. Cover and chill to firm up.

2. Meanwhile, bring a large pan of water to the boil. Add the corn, cover to bring back to the boil, then simmer, half-covered, for about 10 minutes until tender. Drain well.

3. Heat the oil in a large frying pan or griddle over a medium heat. Cook the steaks for 3–4 minutes on each side for medium-rare (4–5 minutes for medium).

4. Divide the corn and steaks among four warm plates and top with the chilled butter. Serve immediately, with a mixed green salad.

Easy Chicken Casserole

shopping list

- 1 fresh rosemary sprig
- 2 bay leaves
- 1 small chicken
- 1 red onion, cut into wedges
- 2 carrots, cut into chunks

Serves 6

Preparation Time
15 minutes

Cooking Time
50 minutes

- 2 leeks, cut into chunks
- 2 celery sticks, cut into chunks
- 12 baby new potatoes
- 900ml (1½ pints) hot vegetable stock
- 200g (7oz) green beans, trimmed

How to cook

1. Preheat the oven to 180°C (160°C fan oven) mark 4. Put the herbs and chicken in a large ovenproof and flameproof casserole. Add the onion, carrots, leeks, celery, potatoes and stock. Bring to the boil, then cook in the oven for 45 minutes or until the chicken is cooked. To test the chicken is cooked, pierce the thickest part of the leg with a knife; the juices should run clear.

2. Add the beans and cook for 5 minutes. Spoon the vegetables into six bowls. Carve the chicken and divide among the bowls, and ladle the stock over.

Orange & Chicken Salad

shopping list

- 50g (2oz) cashew nuts
- zest and juice of 2 oranges
- 2 tbsp marmalade
- 1 tbsp honey
- 1 tbsp oyster sauce

Serves 4

Preparation Time
15 minutes

Cooking Time
10 minutes

- 400g (14oz) roast chicken, shredded
- a handful of chopped raw vegetables, such as cucumber, carrot, red and yellow pepper and Chinese leaves

How to cook

1 Put the cashew nuts in a frying pan and cook for 2–3 minutes until golden. Tip into a large serving bowl.

2 To make the dressing, put the orange zest and juice into the frying pan with the marmalade, honey and oyster sauce. Bring to the boil, stirring, then simmer for 2 3 minutes until slightly thickened.

3 Add the roast chicken to the serving bowl with the chopped raw vegetables. Pour the dressing over the salad, toss everything together and serve immediately.

Mushroom, Bacon & Leek Risotto

shopping list

- 25g (1oz) dried mushrooms
- 250g (9oz) dry-cure smoked bacon, rind removed, chopped
- 3 leeks, chopped

Serves 4

Preparation Time
10 minutes

Cooking Time
about 30 minutes

- 300g (11oz) arborio rice
- 20g (¾oz) chives, chopped
- 25g (1oz) freshly grated Parmesan, plus extra to serve

How to cook

1. Put the mushrooms in a large heatproof bowl and pour in 1.4 litres (2½ pints) boiling water. Leave to soak for 10 minutes.

2. Meanwhile, fry the bacon and leeks in a large pan – no need to add oil – for 7–8 minutes until soft and golden.

3. Stir in the rice, cook for 1–2 minutes, then add the mushrooms and their soaking liquor. Cook at a gentle simmer, stirring occasionally, for 15–20 minutes until the rice is cooked and most of the liquid has been absorbed.

4. Stir in the chives and grated Parmesan, then sprinkle with extra Parmesan to serve.

Speedy Beef Noodles

shopping list

- 250g (9oz) fine egg noodles
- 4 tbsp sesame oil, plus a little extra to brush
- 300g (11oz) beef fillet
- 4 tbsp chilli soy sauce
- juice of 1 lime

Serves 4

Preparation Time
5 minutes

Cooking Time
10 minutes

- 2 red peppers, halved, seeded and cut into thin strips
- 200g (7oz) mangetouts, sliced
- 4 tbsp freshly chopped coriander

How to cook

1. Put the noodles in a large bowl and cover with boiling water. Leave to soak for 4 minutes, then rinse under cold running water and set aside.

2. Meanwhile, brush a large frying pan or griddle with a little sesame oil and heat until hot. Fry the beef for 3–4 minutes on each side, or 4–5 minutes if you like it well done. Remove from the pan and keep warm.

3. Add the 4 tbsp sesame oil to the pan with the chilli soy sauce, lime juice, red peppers, mangetouts and coriander and stir to mix. Add the noodles and use two large spoons to toss them over the heat to combine with the sauce and warm through.

4. Cut the beef into thin slices and serve on a bed of noodles.

Aubergine Parmigiana

shopping list

- 2 large aubergines, thinly sliced lengthways
- 2 tbsp olive oil, plus extra to brush
- 3 fat garlic cloves, sliced
- 2 x 200ml tubs fresh Napoletana sauce
- 4 ready-roasted red peppers, roughly chopped
- 20g (¾ oz) fresh basil, roughly chopped

Serves 4

Preparation Time
10 minutes

Cooking Time
about 25 minutes

- 150g (5oz) Taleggio or fontina
  cheese, coarsely grated
- 50g (2oz) Parmesan, coarsely grated
- salt and ground black pepper
- green salad to serve

How to cook

1. Preheat the oven to 200°C (180°C fan oven) mark 6, and preheat the grill until hot. Put the aubergines on an oiled baking sheet, brush with oil, scatter with the garlic and season with salt and pepper. Grill for 5–6 minutes until golden.

2. Spread a little Napoletana sauce over the bottom of an oiled ovenproof dish, then cover with a layer of aubergine and peppers, packing the layers together as tightly as you can Sprinkle a little basil and some of each cheese over the top. Repeat the layers, finishing with a layer of cheese. Season with pepper. Cook in the oven for 20 minutes or until golden. Serve hot with a green salad.

Pumpkin with Chickpeas

shopping list

- ☐ 900g (2lb) pumpkin or squash, such as butternut, crown prince or kabocha, peeled, seeded and chopped into roughly 2cm (¾ in) cubes
- ☐ 1 garlic clove, crushed
- ☐ 2 tbsp olive oil
- ☐ 2 x 400g cans chickpeas, drained

Serves 6

Preparation Time
15 minutes

Cooking Time
25–30 minutes

- 1 2 red onion, thinly sliced
- 1 large bunch coriander, roughly chopped
- salt and ground black pepper
- steamed spinach to serve

For the tahini sauce
- 1 large garlic clove, crushed
- 3 tbsp tahini paste
- juice of 1 lemon

How to cook

1. Preheat the oven to 220°C (200°C fan oven) mark 7. Toss the squash or pumpkin in the garlic and oil, and season. Put in a roasting tin and roast for 25 minutes or until soft.

2. Meanwhile, put the chickpeas in a pan with 150ml (1/4 pint) water over a medium heat, to warm through.

3. To make the tahini sauce, put the garlic in a bowl, add a pinch of salt, then whisk in the tahini paste. Add the lemon juice and 4–5 tbsp cold water – enough to make a consistency between single and double cream – and season.

4. Drain the chickpeas, put in a large bowl, then add the pumpkin, onion and coriander. Pour on the tahini sauce and toss carefully. Adjust the seasoning and serve while warm, with spinach.

Egg & Bacon Tarts

- 500g pack shortcrust pastry, thawed if frozen
- 6 rashers smoked streaky bacon
- 6 medium eggs
- 3 tbsp freshly chopped flat-leafed parsley

Serves 6

Preparation Time
20 minutes, plus
10 minutes chilling

Cooking Time
25 minutes

How to cook

1. Preheat the oven to 200°C (180°C fan oven) mark 6 and put two baking sheets into the oven to heat up.

2. Divide the pastry into six pieces, then roll out and use to line six 10cm (4in) fluted flan tins. Prick the bases with a fork. Cover with greaseproof paper, fill with baking beans and chill for 10 minutes.

3. Put the tart tins on to the preheated baking sheets and bake blind for 10 minutes. Remove the paper and beans and cook for a further 5 minutes or until the pastry is dry. Remove the cases from the oven and increase the temperature to 220°C (200°C fan oven) mark 7.

4. Put a rasher of raw bacon across the base of each tart. Crack the eggs into a cup one at a time, adding one to each tart. Season and cook for 10 minutes until the egg white has set. Sprinkle with parsley to serve.

Poached Thai Salmon

shopping list

- [ ] 200g (7oz) Thai jasmine rice
- [ ] 1 tbsp sesame oil
- [ ] 1 red chilli, seeded and finely chopped
- [ ] 5cm (2in) piece fresh root ginger, peeled and finely chopped
- [ ] 1 garlic clove, crushed

Serves 4

Preparation Time
10 minutes

Cooking Time
15 minutes

- 1–2 tbsp miso paste
- 2 tsp Thai fish sauce
- 4 skinless salmon fillets, about 150g (5oz) each
- 150g (5oz) fresh shiitake mushrooms, sliced
- 250g (9oz) pak choi, roughly chopped
- 100g (3½oz) baby leaf spinach
- 1 lime, quartered

How to cook

1 Put the rice into a small pan with 400ml (14fl oz) boiling water. Cover, bring to the boil, then reduce the heat to low. Cook according to the pack instructions.

2 Heat the sesame oil in a large shallow pan or wok, add the chilli, ginger and garlic and cook for 1–2 minutes. Add the miso paste and fish sauce, then pour over 500ml (18fl oz) hot water.

3 Add the salmon and mushrooms, then cover and simmer for 7–8 minutes until fish is just cooked. Steam the pak choi and spinach over boiling water for 4–5 minutes. Serve the salmon with some of the sauce, with the rice, vegetables and lime wedges to squeeze over.

Chicken with Spicy Couscous

shopping list

- ☐ 125g (4oz) couscous
- ☐ 1 ripe mango, peeled, stoned and cut into 2.5cm (1in) chunks
- ☐ 1 tbsp lemon or lime juice
- ☐ 125g tub fresh tomato salsa

Serves 4

Preparation Time
15 minutes,
plus 15 minutes
soaking

- 3 tbsp mango chutney
- 3 tbsp orange juice
- 2 tbsp freshly chopped coriander, plus extra to garnish
- 200g pack char-grilled chicken fillets

- 4 tbsp fromage frais
- salt and ground black pepper
- lime wedges to garnish

How to cook

1 Put the couscous in a large bowl, pour over 300ml (1/2 pint) boiling water, season well with salt and pepper, and leave to stand for 15 minutes.

2 Put the mango chunks on a plate and sprinkle with the lemon or lime juice.

3 Mix together the tomato salsa, mango chutney, orange juice and coriander.

4 Drain the couscous if necessary, fluff the grains with a fork, then stir in the salsa mixture and check the seasoning. Turn out on to a large serving dish, and arrange the chicken and mango on top.

5 Just before serving, spoon the fromage frais over the chicken, and garnish with chopped coriander and lime wedges.

Smoked Fish Pie

shopping list

- [ ] 700g (1½lb) floury potatoes, such as Maris Piper, peeled and chopped
- [ ] 25g (1oz) butter
- [ ] 1 tbsp plain flour
- [ ] ½ onion, finely sliced

Serves 4

Preparation Time
15 minutes

Cooking Time
45–50 minutes

- ☐ 75ml (3fl oz) double cream
- ☐ 150ml (¼ pint) hot vegetable stock
- ☐ a splash of white wine (optional)
- ☐ 15g (½oz) freshly grated Parmesan
- ☐ 2 tsp Dijon mustard
- ☐ 350g (12oz) undyed skinless smoked haddock, roughly chopped
- ☐ 150g (5oz) frozen peas
- ☐ salt and ground black pepper

How to cook

1 Put the potatoes into a pan of cold salted water and bring to the boil. Simmer for 15–20 minutes until tender. Drain well, tip back into the pan, then mash with 15g (½oz) butter. Season with salt and pepper.

2 Preheat the oven to 220°C (200°C fan) mark 7. Heat the remaining butter in a large pan, add the flour and onion, and cook for 10 minutes or until the onion is soft and golden. Add the cream, stock, wine, if using, Parmesan and mustard. Stir everything together and season.

3 Add the fish and peas, and turn off the heat. Stir the mixture carefully.

4 Put the fish mixture into a 2.3 litre (4 pint) ovenproof dish. Cover with the mash, then cook in the oven for 15–20 minutes until the fish is cooked through.

Mozzarella, Ham & Rocket Pizza

shopping list

- a little plain flour to dust
- 290g pack pizza base mix
- 350g (12oz) fresh tomato and chilli pasta sauce
- 250g (9oz) buffalo mozzarella cheese, drained and roughly chopped

Serves 4

Preparation Time
10 minutes

Cooking Time
15–18 minutes

- 6 slices Parma ham, torn into strips
- 50g (2oz) rocket
- a little extra virgin olive oil to drizzle
- salt and ground black pepper

How to cook

1. Preheat the oven to 200°C (180°C fan oven) mark 6 and lightly flour two large baking sheets. Mix up the pizza base according to the pack instructions. Divide the dough into two and knead each ball on a lightly floured surface for about 5 minutes, then roll them out to make two 23cm (9in) rounds. Put each on to the prepared baking sheet.

2. Divide the tomato sauce between the pizza bases and spread it over, leaving a small border around each edge. Scatter over the mozzarella pieces, then scatter with ham Season well with salt and pepper.

3. Cook the pizzas for 15–18 minutes until golden. Slide on to a wooden board, top with rocket leaves and drizzle with olive oil. Cut in half to serve.

Chicken Fajitas

shopping list

- 4 skinless chicken breasts, about 700g (1½ lb) total weight, cut into chunky strips
- 2 tbsp fajita seasoning
- 1 tbsp sunflower oil
- 1 red pepper, seeded and sliced
- 360g jar fajita sauce

Serves 4

Preparation Time
10 minutes

Cooking Time
10 minutes

- 1 bunch of spring onions, trimmed and halved
- 8 large flour tortillas
- 150g (5oz) tomato salsa
- 125g (4oz) guacamole dip
- 150ml (¼ pint) soured cream

How to cook

1. Put the chicken breasts in a shallow dish and toss together with the fajita seasoning. Heat the oil in a large non-stick frying pan, add the chicken and cook for 5 minutes or until golden brown and tender.

2. Add the red pepper and cook for 2 minutes. Pour in the fajita sauce, bring to the boil and simmer for 5 minutes or until thoroughly heated. Add a splash of boiling water if the sauce becomes too thick. Stir in the spring onions and cook for 2 minutes.

3. Meanwhile, warm the tortillas in a microwave on full power for 45 seconds, or wrap in foil and warm in a preheated oven at 180°C (160°C fan oven) mark 4 for 10 minutes.

4. Transfer the chicken to a serving dish and take to the table, along with the tortillas, salsa, guacamole and soured cream. Let everyone help themselves.

Potato & Chorizo Tortilla

shopping list

- 6 tbsp olive oil
- 450g (1lb) potatoes, very thinly sliced
- 225g (8oz) onions, thinly sliced
- 2 garlic cloves, finely chopped

Serves 4

Preparation Time
5 minutes

Cooking Time
25 minutes

- 50g (2oz) sliced chorizo, cut into thin strips
- 6 large eggs, lightly beaten
- salt and ground black pepper

How to cook

1. Heat the oil in an 18cm (7in) non-stick frying pan over a medium-low heat. Add the potatoes, onions and garlic. Stir together until coated in the oil, then cover the pan. Cook gently, stirring from time to time, for 10–15 minutes until the potato is soft. Season with salt, then add the chorizo.

2. Preheat the grill until hot. Season the beaten eggs with salt and pepper, and pour over the potato mixture. Cook over a medium heat for 5 minutes or until beginning to brown at the edges and the egg is about three-quarters set.

3. Put the pan under the grill to brown the top. The egg should be a little soft in the middle, as it continues to cook and set as it cools.

4. Carefully loosen the tortilla around the edge and underneath with a flexible turner or spatula. Cut into wedges and serve.

Sticky Chicken Thighs

shopping list

- ☐ 1 garlic clove, crushed
- ☐ 1 tbsp clear honey
- ☐ 1 tbsp Thai sweet chilli sauce
- ☐ 4 chicken thighs
- ☐ green salad to serve

Serves 4

Preparation Time
5 minutes

Cooking Time
20 minutes

How to cook

1. Preheat the oven to 200°C (180°C fan oven) mark 6. Put the garlic into a bowl with the honey and chilli sauce and mix together. Add the chicken thighs and toss to coat.

2. Put into a roasting tin and roast for 15–20 minutes until the chicken is golden and cooked through. Serve with a crisp green salad.

Cook's Tip

Why not try this recipe with sausages instead of chicken? You could also replace the dressing with a honey and mustard marinade. Make this by mixing together 2 tbsp grain mustard, 3 tbsp clear honey and the grated zest and juice of 1 lemon.

Other titles available:

First published in Great Britain in 2009
by Collins & Brown
10 Southcombe Street
London W14 0RA

An imprint of Anova Books Company Ltd
www.anovabooks.com

The Good Housekeeping website is:
www.allaboutyou.com/goodhousekeeping

ISBN 978-1-84340-559-7

The recipes in this book have been chosen
from titles in the Good Housekeeping
Easy to Make! series.

A catalogue record for this book is available
from the British Library.

Reproduction by Dot Gradations Ltd, UK
Printed and bound by Graphicom, Italy

Photography by Nicki Dowey (pages 2, 4,
20, 22, 24, 34, 36, 38, 44, 46, 48, 58 and
62); Craig Robertson (pages 6, 18, 26, 28,
30, 40, 42, 48, 52 and 60); Lucinda Symons
(pages 8, 12, 32 and 56); Neil Barclay
(pages 14 and 50); Martin Brigdale (pages
10 and 16).